Reading W
Imaginary V

LEVEL 5

A ring in the sand

Damian Morgan

Series Editor – Jean Conteh

MACMILLAN

To the Teacher or Parent

This is an imaginary story about three children who find an unusual ring on the beach near their village. After this, their lives begin to improve. Is it the power of the ring, or is it something else that makes their lives better? Readers must decide for themselves.

The story has five chapters.

The book is meant for children to read on their own. The language is clear and simple, and the pictures will help them understand the story.

Use the book like this:

- Before the children begin to read the book, let them look at the picture on the cover. Ask them what they think the title means, and what they think the book might be about.

- Talk with the children about things they find difficult to do, and ways that they may be able to overcome their difficulties.

- Let the children read the book by themselves. Encourage them to work out new words for themselves, and to ask for help if they have problems.

- When the children have finished reading, ask them to turn to pages 39–40, where there are some questions and activities to help them understand the story better.

Above all, let the children enjoy reading this book. Then they will want to read more, and so develop into independent readers.

Chapter 1
Lucky needs to practise

Lucky, Dino and Gloria were friends. They lived near the sea. They were in the same class at school. After school, they often went to the beach.

One day, they were all together on the beach. They all felt a little sad. They sat together for some time, without talking, looking at the sea.

Then, Lucky sighed.

'I'll never be a runner.'

70 – 75

Dino and Gloria were surprised.

Dino said, 'But Lucky! You're a good runner!'

'I mean, I will never be a champion,' Lucky said. 'I should have won the race today.'

He shook his head.

Gloria clapped her hands.

'You're young, Lucky. One day you will be the school champion. Give yourself time,' she told him.

Lucky said, 'No. The problem is, I'm lazy. I must practise running every morning, but some days I stay in bed. I must practise running in the evenings, but some days I sit under the trees. I'm lazy.'

They decided to go home.

But, just as they were leaving, Lucky noticed a patch of rough sand where someone had been digging. He took a stick, and dug into the sand.

His stick struck something solid. He dug with his fingers and found a ring. It was dirty, so he carried it to the sea and washed it.

The ring was smooth and copper-brown.

Lucky slipped it onto the middle finger of his left hand. It was a perfect fit!

Lucky ran up the track back to the village and called, 'Gloria! Dino! Look at this ring!'

But they were too far ahead, and didn't hear him.

He ran home. His mother was cooking the evening meal.

He was so happy with the ring that he ran right around the village, three times. When he came home, the rest of the family had already eaten their meal.

The next morning, Lucky woke early, before the sun was up. He touched the ring and jumped out of bed. Once again, he ran around the village three times. Then he ran home and ate his breakfast.

His mother said, 'You're running well, Lucky!'

Lucky grinned.

'Running is fun.'

As he ran to school that morning, Lucky decided the other children would laugh at the ring.

He tried to slip it free from his finger. But the ring was too tight. He stopped at a tap and wet his finger. He wriggled and pulled at the ring, but it would not slip from his finger.

He ran to school. At breaktime, he ran right round the school three times.

After school, Dino said, 'My mother wants me to go to the market, Lucky. I have no energy. Will you go for me?'

Dino had been very ill the year before. Now he had no appetite for food, and no energy.

Lucky felt sorry for Dino, but he shook his head.

'I have to run four times round the village before dinner,' he said.

At lunchtime the next day, Gloria said to Lucky,
'Do you think I look good?'

'Sure,' Lucky replied.

'Do I have an attractive face?'

'Yes, you do,' Lucky said.

He did not want to spend time answering questions,
as he wanted to run around the school field.

But Gloria didn't stop asking questions.

'Do I dress well?' she asked.

'Yes, Gloria, you do. Why are you asking me all these questions?' said Lucky.

'You know I want to be a model. Do you think I will ever get a chance?'

'I'm sure you will, one day,' Lucky told her.

Lucky ran around the school buildings.

He thought about Gloria.

'She'll never be a model,' he thought. 'She's much too shy. She doesn't have enough confidence.'

Lucky practised running every morning.
He practised running every evening.
His body became as lean as a pencil.
His face became sharp and his eyes were clear.
At the end of the month, he entered the district running championship. Gloria and Dino travelled on the bus to the championship, to keep him company.

Lucky ran like the wind.

He ran fast for the first lap, so he was close to the lead. He ran faster for the second lap and faster for the third lap of the field. By the time he crossed the finishing line, he was five seconds in front of the next runner.

Dino shook his hand, and Gloria slapped his back.

'Now you are a champion runner, Lucky!' she said.

Chapter 2

Gloria needs confidence

The friends got on to the bus to go home.

Lucky was tired.

He fell asleep. His left arm flopped across the seat, and the ring slipped from his finger. It rattled to the floor.

Gloria bent down and picked up the ring.

She wiped the dust from it, and saw how smooth and beautiful it was.

She slipped it onto the middle finger of her left hand.

It was a perfect fit. She decided not to wake Lucky to give it back to him.

'I'll keep it safe on my finger, and give it back to him tomorrow,' she thought.

When Gloria reached school the next day, her teacher said, 'Gloria! You look so good. Look at your straight back! You have the straightest back in the school!'

At lunchtime, Gloria saw Lucky.

She decided to give him the copper ring. But when she tried to take it from her finger, it wouldn't come off!

In the afternoon another teacher said, 'Gloria, does a special dressmaker make your clothes?'

'Oh no,' Gloria said. 'My mother buys them from the tailor.'

'They fit you so well,' said the teacher, 'and when I saw you on Sunday, in your best clothes, you looked so smart!'

Gloria smiled. She felt so confident.

The next day, the headteacher walked into the classroom.

She asked to see Gloria. She spoke to her in the corridor.

'Gloria, our school has been judged the best looked-after school in the district. I'm going into the city to accept our prize from the Minister. Would you like to come with me?'

Gloria stood straight and tall.

'Yes, ma'am. I'd love to!' she replied.

The next morning, Gloria was very excited.

She dressed very carefully in her school uniform. On the way to the city, she sat beside the headteacher in her car. She felt very confident. Hundreds of people packed the city hall.

The Minister shook Gloria's hand.

'Your school has done a wonderful job!' he said. 'It's an example to schools all over the country.'

A man took a photograph of the Minister shaking Gloria's hand.

Gloria smiled, and showed her beautiful white teeth. She felt so happy she wanted to sing and dance right there in front of all the people!

Lunch was set out on tables. Gloria was so excited that she couldn't eat.

A man came up to her.

First, he spoke to Gloria's headteacher. Then he gave Gloria a small business card.

'I run a modelling agency,' he explained. 'We need a picture of a girl your age for the cover of *Health* magazine. I think you have the face we are looking for.'

Gloria held the man's little card.

She whispered, 'I would love to be a model.'

The next day, at school, Gloria told Lucky and Dino about the man from the modelling agency.

She said, 'Will you come with me? I have to meet the photographer after school. My mum will be there, too.'

Lucky said, 'I have to practise running. I'm sorry, Gloria.'

Dino sighed.

'I want to, Gloria, but I have no energy.'

Lucky said, 'You have no energy because you never eat!'

Dino sighed again.

'It's true. But since my illness, I have no appetite. What can I do?' he asked.

Gloria's face was on the next issue of *Health* magazine. Everyone thought she looked beautiful.

A few weeks later, she got another letter from the modelling agency. A large clothing company wanted Gloria to model their clothes for girls. The agency asked her to come to the city, to have photographs taken.

Gloria's mother went with her to the city. They stayed in a hotel, which the modelling agency paid for.

Gloria dressed in new clothes and walked, danced, ran and skipped amongst the trees in a garden, while the photographer took picture after picture.

By the end of the day, she was so tired that she fell straight to sleep, with a smile on her face.

Her dreams had come true.

When she went back to school the next day, Gloria was very tired.

During the first lesson, she dropped her head onto the desk and fell asleep.

Her left arm slipped. The copper ring slid from her finger and rattled to the floor.

Chapter 3

Dino needs to eat

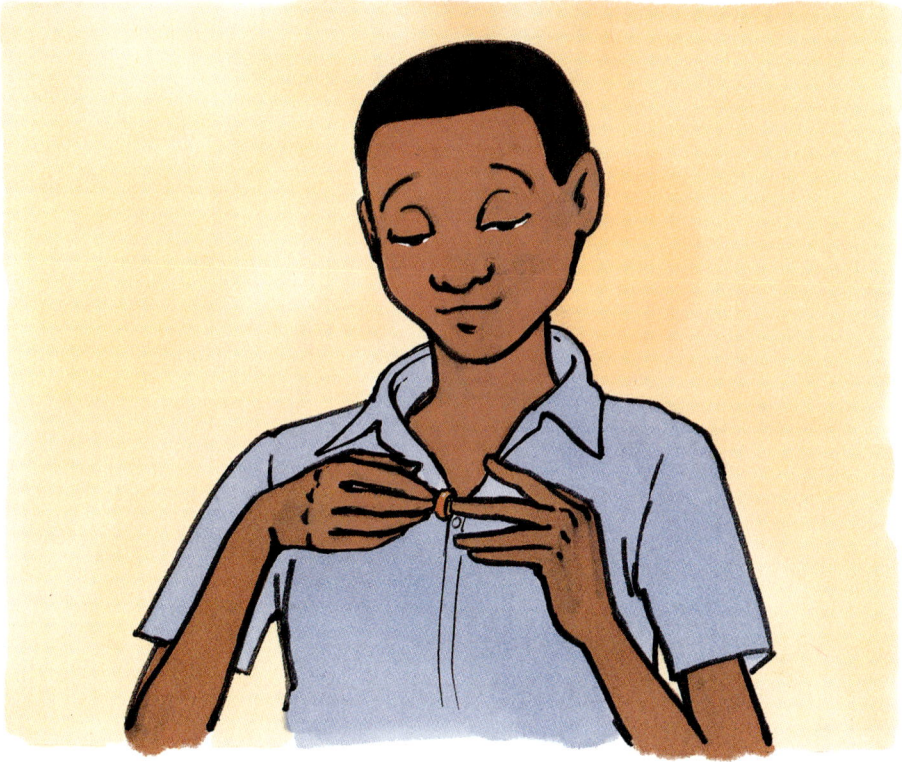

Dino heard the ring fall to the floor.

He reached down and picked it up. He saw that the ring was beautiful. He slid it onto the middle finger of his left hand.

The ring was a perfect fit! But when he wriggled the ring to take it off, it wouldn't move.

At lunchtime, Dino felt very hungry.
He took a banana from his bag and ate it.
He was still hungry.
He watched his friends eating.
He looked so hungry that Gloria gave him some cake and Lucky gave him some bread. He ate them and felt better.
During the afternoon, he felt a surge of energy. For the first time for over a year, he worked hard at his lessons.

When Dino reached home, his mother looked in his bag.

'Where's your banana, Dino?' she asked. 'You didn't sell it, did you?'

'I ate it,' Dino told her.

His mother was surprised.

'You never eat your lunch!'

She felt happy, as she had been worried about her son.

Dino still felt hungry, so he ate two more bananas. When his mother finished cooking the evening meal, he ate everything on his plate, and then had a second helping.

'You are a good boy!' said his mother.

Dino said, 'Is there any more?'

Later, Dino walked down the road. A man was selling hamburgers from a stall.

Dino bought one, and ate it. It tasted beautiful!

When he got home, he tried to wriggle the ring to get it off his finger.

He rubbed soap on his finger to make the skin slippery. The ring would still not come off.

He felt guilty.

What would he say to Gloria?

For breakfast the next morning, Dino ate two large bowls of porridge. All morning, he worked hard at his studies.

For lunch, he ate five large bananas. On the way home from school, he stopped at the food stall again, and bought another hamburger.

Then he ran with Lucky, but he could not keep up with him.

The next day, he went into the town with Gloria and her mother. Gloria was doing some more modelling. Dino ate two packets of crisps while the photographer took pictures of Gloria.

Two weeks later, Dino's mother said, 'Dino, come into town with me. You've grown so big that none of your clothes fit you.'

Dino's mother asked the tailor to make Dino new trousers and a new shirt. Although Dino ate all the time, his mother was happy.

He was no longer weak and thin. He helped her in the house. He swept the yard, he took messages for her, he worked hard at school. Dino was a boy to be proud of!

Chapter 4
Will Dino stop eating?

One day, a month later, Gloria met Lucky after school.

'Come to the beach,' she said. 'I want to talk to you.'

Lucky said, 'I have to practise running.'

'No, Lucky,' replied Gloria. 'This is important. Come with me.'

The two friends walked to the beach. They sat together on the sand.

Gloria said, 'Do you remember the copper ring you found in the sand?'

Lucky said, 'I don't know where it went.'

Gloria said, 'I'm sorry, Lucky. I took it.'

Lucky didn't say anything.

Gloria went on.

'I wanted to be a model, but I was too shy. I put on your ring and, suddenly, I felt confident. People noticed me. I got lots of modelling jobs. One day I realised the ring had gone, but it didn't matter. I wasn't shy any more.'

Lucky said, 'When I put the ring on, all I wanted to do was run. One day, I looked at my finger and the ring had gone. It didn't matter. I found I loved running so much, I didn't need the ring any more.'

Gloria said, 'The ring fell off your finger on the bus. That's when I put it on. I wanted to keep it safe for you, but then it wouldn't come off.'

Lucky said, 'Dino is wearing the ring now.'

'He must have picked it up when it fell from my finger,' said Gloria.

Lucky said, 'That's why he's eating now. He has lots of energy. Look how well he's doing at school! He's top of the class!'

'But Lucky, shouldn't the ring have fallen from his finger by now?' asked Gloria. 'He just keeps eating and eating. Yesterday he broke the chair he was sitting on.'

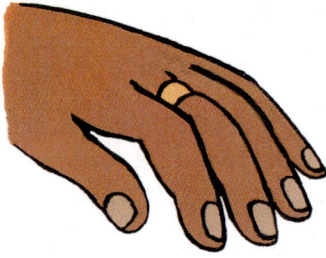

Lucky whispered, 'His finger's so fat, the ring can't slip off.'

'What are we going to do? If he keeps eating like this, he'll explode!' said Gloria.

Lucky stared at his friend. Gloria was right. Lucky and Gloria made a plan.

After school the next day, Gloria and Dino ran with Lucky along the beach. They ran a long way, until they came to an old hut that used to belong to a fisherman.

Dino gasped for breath.

He said, 'I like running, but I'm too fat to run this far!'

Lucky said, 'Come into the hut and sit down for a moment.'

As soon as Dino was sitting down, Lucky and Gloria hurried outside and slammed the door.

Dino called, 'What are you doing?'

Gloria said, 'You're staying in the hut until you lose some weight!'

Lucky snapped the lock shut.

After school the next day, Lucky ran to the hut.
Dino called, 'Lucky, I'm so, so hungry!'
'Can you take the ring off?' asked Lucky.
'No,' said Dino, sadly.
'So, you're on a diet,' Lucky told him.

He passed some water through a high, small
window, and then a plate with a little food on it.
  'That's all you get!' he told Dino.
  Dino said, 'Aren't people looking for me?'
  'Gloria told your mother that you've gone to stay
with your uncle.'
  'Oh…' Dino moaned. 'I'm so hungry, Lucky!'

The next day, Dino held his hand out the window and Gloria tried to slide the ring from his finger. He had been in the hut for two days, but his finger was still so fat that the ring still didn't move.

Gloria and Lucky visited Dino every day, to bring him water and a little bit of food, and to see if he was all right.

After he had been in the hut for six days, Dino said to Lucky, 'I'm so hungry, hungry, hungry, hungry!'

On the seventh day, Gloria pulled at the ring and it slipped neatly into her hand.

Dino cried, 'Food! Food! Give me food!'

They let Dino out of the hut.

Gloria studied the beautiful copper-coloured ring.

Lucky said, 'Gloria, don't you dare put that ring back on your finger. You don't know what will happen!'

They explained to Dino about the power of the ring.

Dino said, 'Do you have any more bananas?'

When Dino could eat no more, the three friends walked back along the beach.

Gloria held up the copper ring.

'Thank you for giving me confidence,' she said.

Lucky took it in his hand and said, 'Thank you for encouraging me to practise.'

Dino took the ring and said, 'Thank you for giving me an appetite.'

Then Gloria took the ring, and threw it far out into the sea.

Chapter 5

The power of the ring

The next afternoon, a fishing boat was heading towards the beach. The boy in the boat had fished for two hours, but he had caught nothing.

'Sitting in a boat is boring. Maybe I should find some other work,' he sighed.

He pulled in his net for the last time, and found there was only one small fish in it. The fish was hardly big enough for his dinner.

The boy scraped the scales from the fish, cut off the head, and cleaned the fish. A dirty ring fell into his hand.

The boy washed the ring. It gleamed a bright copper colour.

The boy raised his arm to throw the ring back into the sea. But, before he let it go, he changed his mind. He slipped the ring onto the middle finger of his left hand.

It was a perfect fit.

He turned the boat back out to sea.

What do you think happened when he cast his net into the sea?

1. The three friends, Lucky, Gloria and Dino, each had a problem. Write a sentence saying what each child's problem was.

2. Imagine that you are one of the three children. Which child would you choose to be? Imagine that you are putting on the ring for the first time. How do you think it would feel? Which of these words could describe the feeling?

- excited
- sad
- keen
- disappointed
- hopeful
- tired
- lazy
- eager

3. Now imagine that you are writing in your diary about putting on the ring for the first time. What would you write? Take some paper, and write your imaginary diary entry. Use some of the words from Activity 2. You could begin like this:

Today, I put on the beautiful copper ring I found in the sand. I felt...........

Activity page

4 On page **17**, the owner of the modelling agency gave Gloria his business card. Have you ever seen a business card? They are very small, and look something like this:

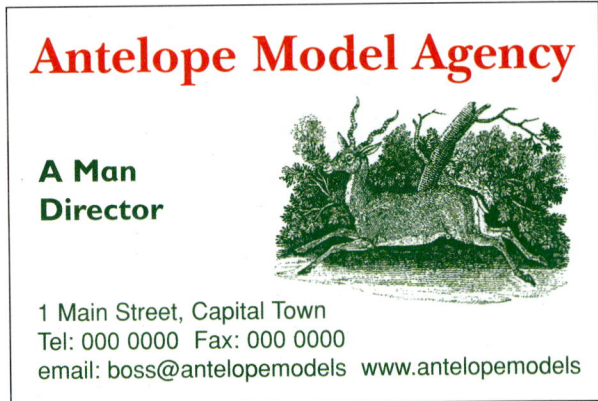

Antelope Model Agency

A Man Director

1 Main Street, Capital Town
Tel: 000 0000 Fax: 000 0000
email: boss@antelopemodels www.antelopemodels

Imagine that you have your own business. Design and draw your own business card.

5 On page **25**, Dino said, 'Is there any more?' after his mother said he was a good boy. Why did Dino say this? Write a list of all the things he had eaten that day.

6 Why did Lucky and Gloria lock Dino in the fisherman's hut? Do you think this was a safe thing to do? Did their plan work? What would you have done, if you were Lucky or Gloria?

7 The story ends with a question. What do you think the answer is?

8 What power do you think the ring has? What would you hope for, if you found the ring and put it on?